Book 3 • Early Intermediate

One of a Kind Solos

9 Unique Piano Pieces
by Wynn-Anne Rossi

Foreword

What does it mean to be one of a kind? Wonderful words and phrases come to mind like *unique*, *original*, *outside-the-box*, even *extraordinary*. These represent values that I have understood since I was a young child. Colorful family stories made it obvious that being different was a good thing! As an adult, I understand these also represent the values of a musician. A performer reaches for special, one-of-a-kind ways to play a piece. A composer explores new territory, discovering one-of-a-kind musical ideas to express emotions, imagination, and the world around us.

One of a Kind Solos represents a very personal journey with music. Some pieces reveal a quirky, playful side. Others delve into the mysterious, exhilarating, or beautiful. Throughout the series, you will discover musical surprises, from humorous lyrics and unusual modes to odd meters and interpretative challenges. This is what I love most about music—the adventure of self-discovery that allows me to be myself. My hope is that these pieces will also guide you in your voyage to being *one of a kind*!

Wynn-Anne Rossi

Contents

Alfred Music
P.O. Box 10003
Van Nuys, CA 91410-0003
alfred.com

ISBN-10: 1-4706-1055-8
ISBN-13: 978-1-4706-1055-5

Cover Photos
Piano ink drawing: © iStockphoto.com / mecaleha • Light grunge scrollwork: © iStockphoto.com / Cloudniners

Morning Prelude

Wynn-Anne Rossi

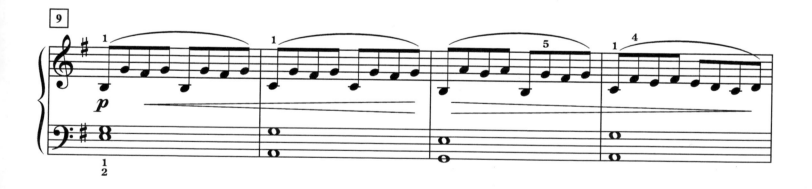

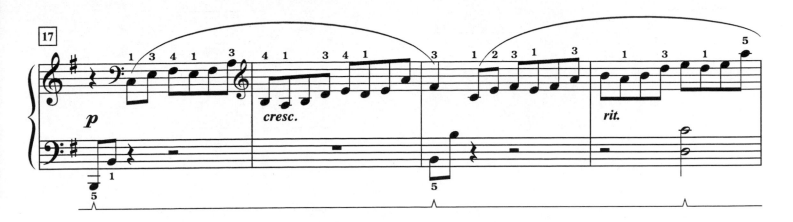

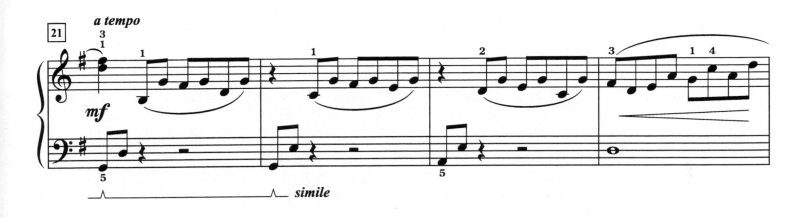

4

Boogie Bash

Wynn-Anne Rossi

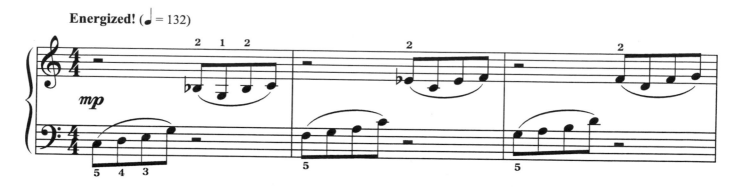

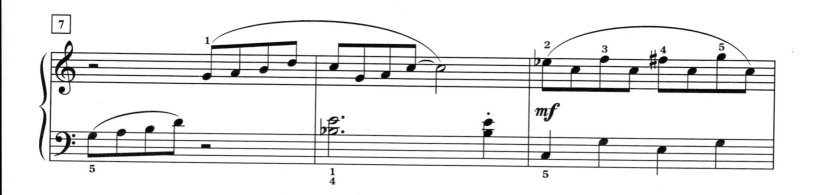

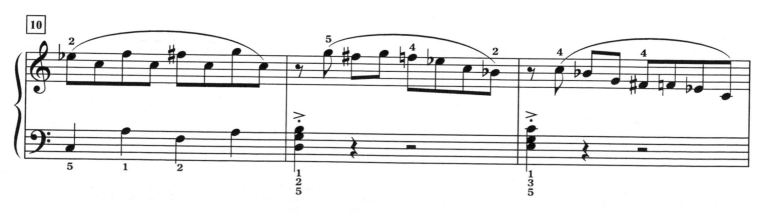

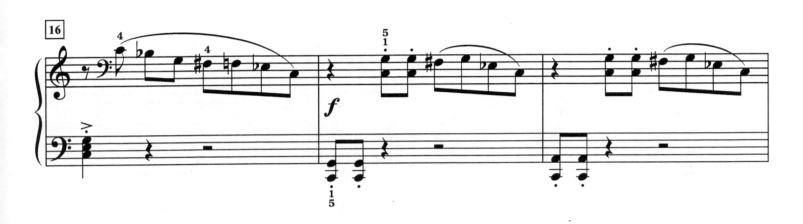

6

Hero Variations

Wynn-Anne Rossi

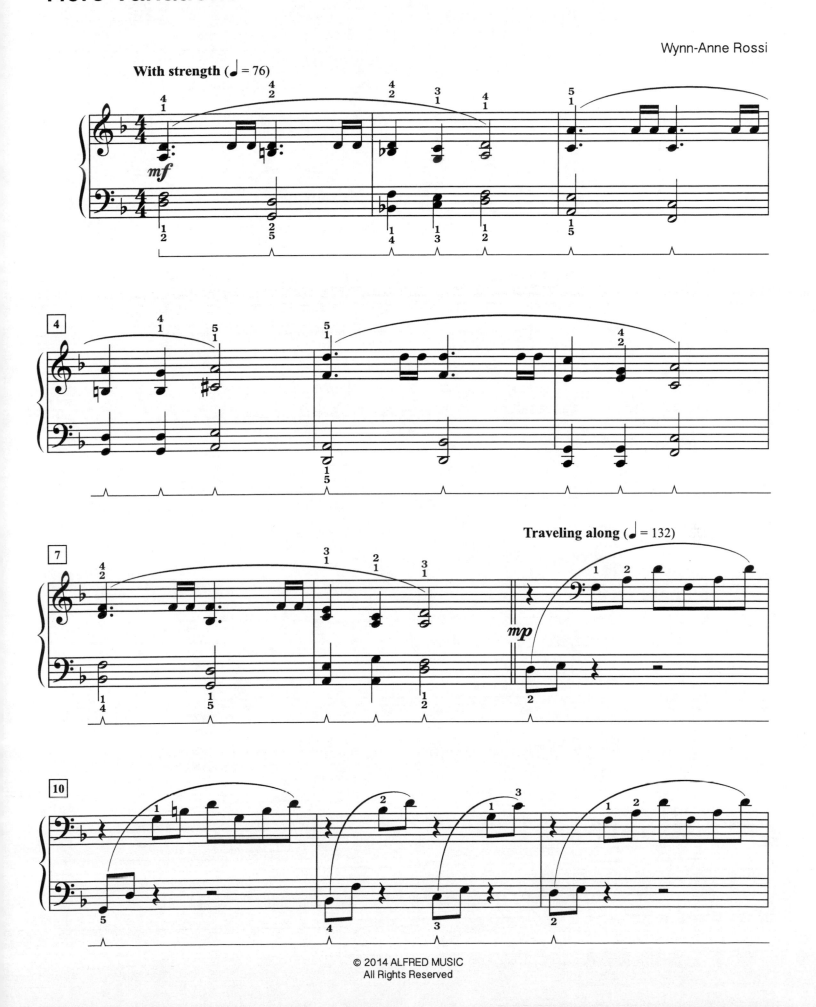

Midnight Snowfall

Wynn-Anne Rossi

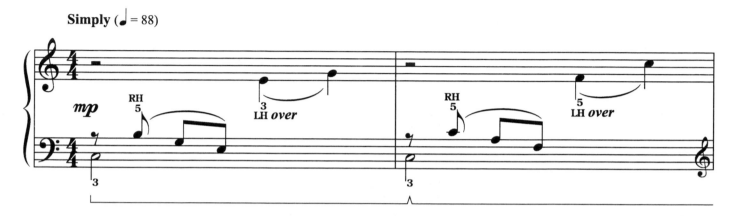

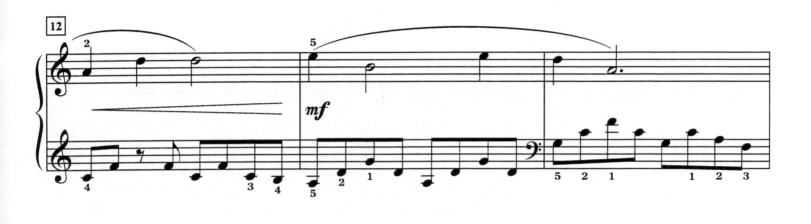

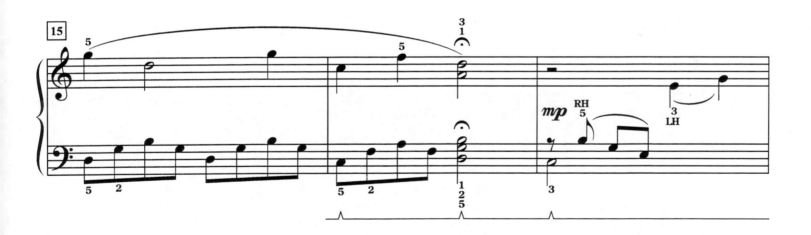

Zingaro Dance *

Wynn-Anne Rossi

* A *zingaro* is an Italian gypsy.

Half Step Jazz

Wynn-Anne Rossi

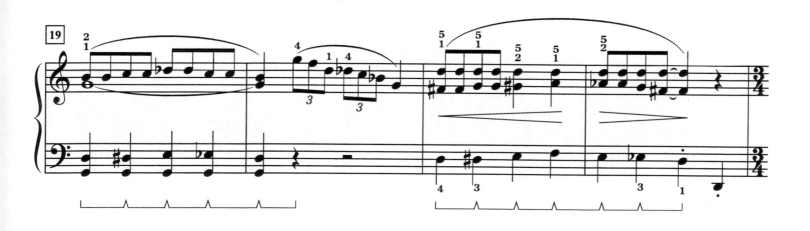

Raise the Barn!

Wynn-Anne Rossi

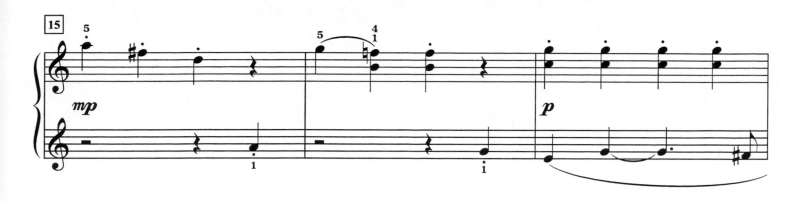

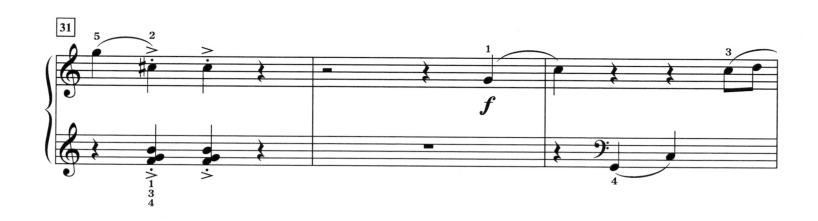

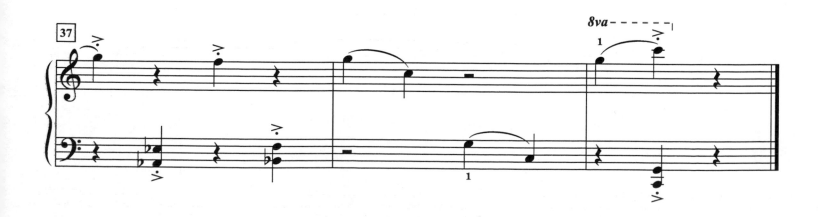

Forever Friends

Wynn-Anne Rossi

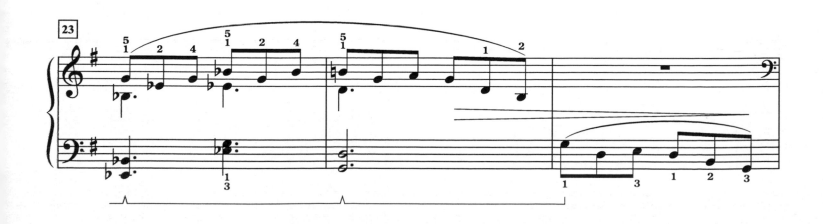

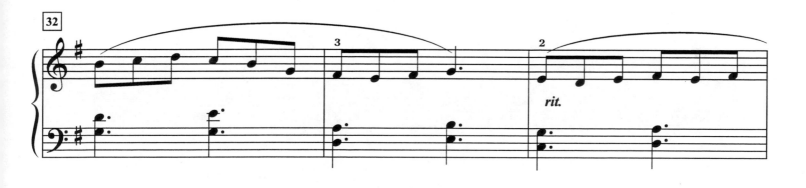

Prankster

Wynn-Anne Rossi